Kirkcudbright

your town in photographs
by Philip Dunn

Squall across Wigtown Bay

Dramatic light and low tide unveil the glory of the unspoiled coastline just a few short miles from Kirkcudbright town centre. That rain storm was heading my way – I got soaked. This is 'Bonnie Galloway' - a very special place.

www.photoactive.co.uk

Published by Philip Dunn 2006
Printed by Stranraer and Wigtownshire Free Press

ISBN 10: 0-9553378-0-1
ISBN 13: 978-0-9553378-0-2

To the people of Kirkcudbright

Seeing your town

This collection of photographs formed my 'Your Kirkcudbright' exhibition at the Tolbooth Art Centre in the town. More pictures have been added here. The response from local people to the exhibition was tremendous. "Where's the book," I was asked. Well here it is - a photographic celebration of your Kirkcudbright, and I am pleased to say it is entirely a product of Bonnie Galloway - it was even printed here.

People are attracted to Kirkcudbright for many reasons, two in particular - the warm nature of the people who live here, and the visual beauty of the town and surrounding countryside. There's something very special here, not least a tremendous sense of community. There is genuine pride in the place and it shows.

Photographers come to me for tuition from right across Britain and Europe. The exhibition - and the book - were born from a desire to say thank you to the Kirkcudbright townsfolk who are always so welcoming to them - many of these clients are discovering Scotland's Artists' Town and Galloway for the first time. Most fall in love with the place and come back again.

During my photography courses, I try to teach people how to 'see' more clearly. I hope this collection of photographs will inspire those who have not really looked closely at their town before, and give even more pleasure to those who have.

PHILIP DUNN

The photograph **above** shows *Wellspring*, the wonderfully picturesque wooden hulk on Dee Walk. See also pages 16-17

Cover photograph shows a detail of the wooden statue on Fishermen's Green.
Back cover - love on the Dhoon.
Opposite page - Kirkcudbright is a town that likes to be spick-and-span.

Left
Brightly-coloured houses in Castle Street, Kirkcudbright – it is sometimes possible to photograph the town AND hide all those parked cars.

Opposite
Autumn leaves at Greyfriars Church. Colours and patterns are all around us – we just need to look more closely to spot them.

Far right, top to bottom
The circus comes to town. Shore House - very nautical. Cranberries gift shop at dusk.

Left
MacLellan's Castle. The dark, brooding silhouette of the castle and a great splosh of gold from the dried grass in the railings.

Right
MacLellan's Castle with the gardens in full summer bloom looks a lot more inviting.

4

5

Right

The tide is going out, and local scallop dredgers *King Explorer* and *Fredwood* dry out beside the quay and beneath MacLellan's castle.

Below

If we look more closely at the things around us, even ugly structures like the concrete bridge and the dairy can have some visual merit - although these two structures are a test for any photographer.

Above

With the quayside almost in total shadow, and the low, golden rays of the winter sun just spot-lighting the concrete bridge, *Solway Ranger* prepares to leave Kirkcudbright on the last of the tide. This sort of light does not last more than a few fleeting moments and a photographer must work very quickly.

Right

Fishermen of all ages use the harbour quayside. Some quite large sea bass have been caught from the quay - but this youngster was out of luck on this particular day. He caught nothing.

7

The shore at Knockbrex, overlooking the islands of Ardwall and Barlocco, is one of my favourite places to take pictures.

I especially like to take photographs there in the late afternoon when there's a strong south-westerly wind blowing and the waves are breaking. My students who come up from London think they are in heaven.

My students are often a little nervous about photographing people, but the folk of Kirkcudbright always make them feel at ease - and the smiles never seem to be a problem.

Lower centre is Gary McKie; boatman, beachcomber, fisherman, storyteller and much more. In the summer months Gary runs the little pleasure boat *The Lovely Nellie*, taking visitors on river trips up and down the River Dee (see page 50).

Far left-centre is Rab Thomson, Harbour Master, who served for many years with the local lifeboat.

Near left is Tom Bernie, a regular volunteer model for my photography students.

Just stand on the quayside for a while and the photographs will come to you. Watch your step, though; this is a busy work place and fishing is a tough job. In the picture (**right**), the skipper looks out of the wheel house of *Azula*. Even after several days at sea, most of the fishermen who unload their scallops here manage to joke and chat with the tourists who point their cameras. The job must teach them a degree of tolerance.

Kirkcudbright is fairly new to the fishing industry - it was not until the 1960s that fishing became a big part of the town's economy. Until then, agriculture, sea trading and some boat building were the mainstays... plus art and tourism, of course.

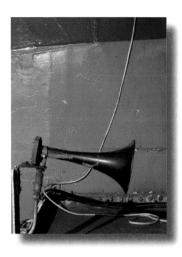

The West Coast Sea Products plant on Dee Walk is a major employer in Kirkcudbright. Scallops landed in the harbour are brought straight here for processing before being despatched to gourmet restaurants and dinner tables all over Britain and Europe.

Kirkcudbright is without doubt the scallop capital of the universe, and the mountain of empty shells from all those queen and king scallops can make great subjects for any photographer.

A bright red ice skip (**right**) is the subject for this geometric and colourful photograph,

14

Some claim that the old wooden hulks of the *Wellspring* and the *Loch Ryan Lady* (**see next pages**) are eyesores, and attempts are made to have them removed from the tidal mud on Dee Walk.

Yet countless photographers take pictures of them and artists can often be seen sketching them. I have taken hundreds of my students to photograph these old boats. Why? Because the hulks have powerful visual appeal for those prepared to see. In the right light, they can be very rewarding to look at. One lady, who worked at The National Theatre in London, told me they had a whole department working to simulate the sort of weathered effect nature is creating on *Wellspring*.

Eyesores more worthy of attention include the tacky street furniture and signage that is proliferating everywhere, ruining many of the best views of your town and countryside. Every few hundred yards along local country lanes, unnecessary and unsightly signage tells cyclists they are on the correctly-numbered cycle route, or that it marks a 'passing place' for cars.

Let's keep things clean, by all means, but this obsessive urge to 'tidy-up' all things old, and label everything with the obvious is depriving us of many worthwhile views and opportunities for visual enrichment. A totally sanitised world will hardly be worth looking at.

The *Loch Ryan Lady* lies quietly falling to bits on the banks of the River Dee. It's sad that this wooden, clinker-built boat will never sail again, but the textures and colours of the flaking paint on the hull are wonderful.

It's best to see her in a variety of different light conditions for the most dramatic effects.

With the afternoon light behind MacLellan's castle and the Tolbooth, the Royal Burgh of Kirkcudbright can boast a very distinctive and attractive skyline. In this light, a time traveller would notice very little change if he paid us a visit from several centuries ago.

The timelessness of this scene is re-enforced by the lobster fisherman rowing ashore after mooring his boat in the middle of the river. He's bringing back his catch, and he'll climb up that mud bank and take it home - an activity our time traveller would certainly recognise.

He'd also recognise the salmon nets (**above**) in the Cree estuary just a few miles from Kirkcudbright. Another activity that goes back hundreds of years.

20

It was a sad day for the town when Dougie Ross retired and closed the doors of his grocery shop for the last time. It was a gem.

Now Dougie is free to spend more time on his little boat, fishing in Kirkcudbright Bay and beyond. In the winter, *Robbern* is tucked-up beneath a tarpaulin cover on the mud beside the river.

The River Dee below Tongland Bridge is a haven for waterfowl and otters. Before the concrete town bridge replaced a swing bridge, trading schooners were able to navigate right up here and there were landing wharfs.

22

Opposite page
   Top left: Thousands of starlings swirling over the town before roosting for the night.
   Top right: Mist comes up river with the tide.
   Left: From the Galloway coast the Isle of Man can be seen clearly on a good day.

This page
   Above: Heading out to sea and into the gathering darkness - the scallop dredger *Aquinas* disturbs the glassy water in the channel of Kirkcudbright Bay.
   Right: Drilling for oil in Kirkcudbright Bay? Nothing so exciting - this rig was working on a new sewer outfall.

Looking back again towards the town from up the twisting River Dee, the riverside grasses and reeds shine golden in the low, winter light (**left**).

The scene changes constantly with the light and tide. At low water, wading birds probe the glittering mud and herons stand to fish every few hundred yards along the banks. As the tide rises and hides the mud banks, shelduck decorate the water.

There is always something to see - and it's all within a few minutes walk of the centre of town.

Carry on further along the footpath that follows the riverbank to Tongland Bridge for views of the river through the trees (**above**).

Far left
The location of the waterfall is a secret; a magical place. The fairy folk who live there have sworn me to secrecy and I do not want to upset them.

Left
If you are going to build a power station - make it look good... and the hydro-electric power station at Tongland certainly does.

Above
The old railway piers have now been demolished. Another example of the tidy-up mania that is destroying much of our visual heritage. The stones now lie in a heap.

29

Over the centuries, it's not just legitimate cargoes of wine, iron, oil, pottery, guano and countless other goods that have been landed at Kirkcudbright Harbour. The harbour's strategic position on the Irish Sea coast made it a perfect haven for smugglers. Much of the smuggled rum, brandy, salt and tobacco came via the Isle of Man.

The first steamship to arrive in port was the *Rob Roy* in 1820. One of the largest vessels to use the quay was a 220ft timber ship in 2002. She was piloted by a retired local fishing skipper. Harbour activity today is centred around the busy fleet of scallop dredgers.

Right
When this photograph showing the distant outline of the ruins of MacLellan's Castle was shown in the 'Your Kirkcudbright' exhibition, I asked visitors to tell me where it was taken from. Not many people got it right. One of the few who did was the man who installed the leaded window!

It was actually taken through an upstairs window in St Cuthbert's Parish Church.

Above
The organ pipes and newly-painted ceiling in the Parish Church

Opposite

   Clockwise from top left: Discarded beach rubbish can be worth looking at sometimes.
The shiny-black frontage of the Masonic Arms in Castle Street.
Sheep get their heads down to the late winter grass near the church at Borgue .

This page

   Right: Spring daffodils on the Moat Brae.

   Below: Port and starboard navigation buoys from the river channel on the quayside for servicing.

   Below right:
This view of Kirkcudbright is always a welcome sight for sailors after a long trip.

I'm not suggesting we should surround ourselves with the sort of decay and dereliction seen in the pictures on this page, even if it does make interesting photographs.

However, the extraordinarily beautiful stricken oak (**opposite**) has now been destroyed in a brutal 'tidy-up' of farm land just outside the town. Several other ancient, and equally beautiful trees, were simply cut down to ground level. They attracted woodpeckers and wildlife and were a visual feast for the eyes.

Next pages
Some old tree stumps and roots that have survived - for the time being...

The piano (**above**) might need a little tuning before it plays its next open-air concert, but the *Titanic* is sailing along merrily in this window (**above right**). And if it comes to a choice of warming my feet on that old electric fire (**centre right**) or that glowing stove (**right**), I know which I'd prefer. The stove, the *Titanic* and the piano were photographed behind a house in the High Street. The electric fire was found in a barn just outside town.

The dusty attic corner (**far right**) was in Wilson Lochhead's Old Mill Pottery. See next pages for more pictures of Wilson and the pottery.

40

Wilson Lochhead's pottery was a treasure chest for any photographer. There were pictures to be captured everywhere - including portraits of Wilson himself, and I often photographed him at work.

Sadly, Wilson, the second generation of Lochheads to produce beautiful and practical studio pots, has now stopped potting at the mill. A great loss to the town - and certainly to photographers.

A big wide sky, a flock of sheep dashing across the rolling countryside, and an old tree - it doesn't need many ingredients to capture the sense of open air, freshness and freedom that is at the very heart of the Galloway landscape.

When they are out with me taking landscape photographs, I try to encourage my students to adopt what I call 'visual agility'. I want them to see more than just the big, overall view, and to notice the less obvious subjects that might be right there at their feet; a frost-dusted leaf or a flower, for instance. All you have to do is look more closely, and you don't need to be a photographer to benefit from this way of seeing.

Galloway is rightly proud of its famous Belted Galloway cattle, or 'belties', as they are known locally, and I was sorely tempted to paint a 'beltie's' white belt on the photo above, but I'm glad I did not. The farmer who owned the animal came to the 'Your Kirkcudbright' photography exhibition and saw this picture. He recognised his beast straight away. "Besides", he told me. "A beltie is a wee bit shorter in the leg - you'd never ha' got away with it."

We may be in the Lowlands of Scotland here in Galloway, but we still have some Highland cattle in the area (**right**).

Cow buoys - these cows (**left**) were attracted to the buoy opposite the yacht pontoon

I make no apologies for including these photographs taken at Wallets Mart auctioneers in Castle Douglas in a book mainly about Kirkcudbright. On rainy days I often take my students to the cattle and sheep sales in Castle Douglas, and the farmers there are always extremely hospitable and helpful.

The best thing is that the farmers and staff mostly just get on with what they are doing - and this always helps create more natural photographs.

The picture **top far right**, shows Wallets auctioneer Stewart Wilson.

The yacht pontoon in Kirkcudbright (**right**) has proved to be a great asset to both local sailors and visitors. It is a beautiful place to keep a boat, or just spend a few relaxing days. Local traders benefit from the extra business it has brought to the town.

Top left
The Lovely Nellie, the river trip boat run by local man Gary McKie (see pages 10-11).

Above
The Harbour Master's launch, pictured dashing up Kirkcudbright Bay from Little Ross Island.

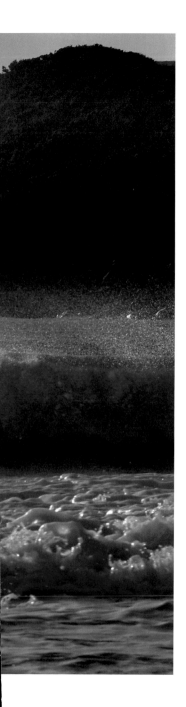

The sailing on the Galloway coast is splendid - far removed from the crowded scramble I used to know on the south coast of England. Here there is space to breathe as well as a magnificent coastline. The picture **above** was taken aboard a boat owned by local author and historian, David Collin, as he headed towards Little Ross Island from Kirkcudbright Bay.

Right
David sails south of the island beneath Little Ross lighthouse.

Left
When the wind blows and the waves break, it's good to stand on the shore at Abbey Burn Foot and look out seawards towards Abbey Head.

The lighthouse on Little Ross Island (**left**) flashes its warning to sailors every five seconds, but there are serious dangers within the relative shelter of Kirkcudbright Bay, and many ships have been wrecked here, especially while trying to cross the bar in a south-easterly blow.

The water is shallow, with submerged rocks and mud banks waiting for the sailor who strays out of the channel at the wrong state of the tide.

The bones of the schooner *Monreith*, (**above**) wrecked in Kirkcudbright Bay in November 1900, still lie off Goatwell Bay, just south of the Dhoon. She was on passage from Northern Ireland to Silloth with a 100 ton cargo of granite kerbstones. All her crew were able to reach the shore in the ship's boat.

In 1960, Little Ross was the scene of violent crime when lighthouse keeper Hugh Clark was murdered by assistant keeper Robert Dickson. The gruesome scene was discovered by local man Thomas Collin and his son David, who landed on the island while out sailing. David still sails in Kirkcudbright Bay and around Little Ross Island (**see previous pages overleaf**). Robert Dickson was found guilty of murder and sentenced to death. He was reprieved, but later hanged himself in prison.

Kirkcudbright churchyard stands on a hill above the town. It is a fascinating place, with many graves dating back to the 1600s.

Here lie hanged Covenanters, ships' captains, local dignitaries and rough-necks alike. People still come to place coins on the gravestone of Billy Marshall, King of the Gypsies, who was said to have been 120 years old when he died in 1792.

Following pages
The Harbour Cottage Gallery photographed at different times of the year.

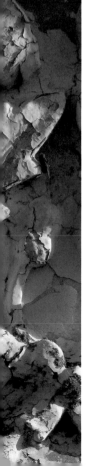

Philip Dunn has been a professional photographer and writer for 40 years

His first picture was published when he was 14 years old. He worked on local and provincial newspapers until the age of 24, when he became the youngest photographer ever to be invited to join the staff of the Daily Express. He remained on the staff for 15 years, then freelanced for the Independent, The Times and The Daily Telegraph, becoming travel photographer for The Sunday Times.

He has been commissioned to write and photograph articles by every top newspaper and magazine in the UK. He has published two books on photography and illustrated many more on other subjects. He has won numerous awards.

Philip now runs photography holidays and courses in Menorca and Kirkcudbright, and makes instructional DVDs on the craft of photography

HIGH QUALITY ART PRINTS OF THE PHOTOGRAPHS IN THIS BOOK

Framed or unframed prints are available of any of the photographs in this book. For details about prints, photography courses and holidays please go to the website

www.photoactive.co.uk

"This exhibition probably demonstrates an active 'third eye' behind the camera, which penetrates to the heart of matter and to the complexity of human motivation. Thank you for giving Kirkcudbright such a marvellous insight and for holding the mirror!"
This comment, and those on the back cover, were written in the visitors' book during the 'Your Kirkcudbright' photography exhibition.

Above
Visitors and locals are all familiar with the wooden sculpture standing on Fishermen's Green in the harbour – but try looking at it in different light conditions - it can look very different at dusk in the fading light of day. The sculpture commemorates all the Kirkcudbright sailors who have lost their lives at sea.

Historical information sourced from:
Kirkcudbright - An Alphabetical Guide to its History by David R. Collin. Published by The Stewartry Museum.